CUSTOMER SERVICE

A One-Act Play

DAVID ZWEIBEL

Cover and interior by Gary A. Rosenberg
www.garyarosenberg.com

Printed in the United States of America.

For Franny

CUSTOMER SERVICE

Cast of Characters

Doctor

Solomon "Sol" Green

Iam

Scene 1

December 1999, Gibbons Regional Hospital, New Jersey,
Fifth Floor Waiting Room

The sound of unintelligible conversation is heard as the curtain rises on a hospital waiting room. The room is small and contains a couch, two chairs, a coffee table littered with old magazines, a fish tank, and a beverage bar. A poor, cheap print with a pastoral theme and a television hang on the wall. A **Doctor** *and* **Mr. Green** *appear at the entrance of the room and have the following exchange before the latter enters by himself.*

Doctor: The laparoscopy shouldn't take very long, Mr. Green. Help yourself to a tea or a coffee. Relax. Remember, this procedure is minimally invasive. You'll be able to see your wife in no time at all.

Sol: Thank you. (*Doctor leaves, Solomon Green is alone in the waiting room.*) Minimally invasive? When it happens to someone else, it's minimally invasive.

Solomon Green, 69, speaks with a slight, barely discernible accent. "Sol" is clearly agitated. He walks over to the beverage bar, picks up a Styrofoam cup and the coffee pot, but decides against having a drink. He then sits down on the couch and grabs a magazine off the coffee table. He opens it, but he cannot concentrate and immediately puts it back. The television then catches his attention and, although the volume is off and the remote control sits just inches away on the table, he just stares blankly at the news broadcast that's in progress.

Soon after, IAM *enters the waiting room. Iam and Sol exchange polite nods. Iam is unkempt, unshaven. He is wearing a tattered, full-length coat. He appears to be Sol's contemporary, but doesn't carry himself with the same air of refinement and self-assuredness. Sol is dressed fashionably, tastefully. Iam takes a seat beside Sol and joins him in watching the TV in silence.*

Sol: *(Remembering his manners.)* Oh, I'm sorry. I'm not really watching. Feel free to put on anything you like.

Iam: *(With a Yiddish accent.)* You're sure? *(Without waiting for an answer* Iam *grabs the remote and quickly changes the channel, eventually stopping at a* Road Runner *cartoon. He also cranks up the volume.)* I love these cartoons. They're so clever. Beep, beep!

Sol looks curiously at the man sitting beside him. At first he thinks it's odd that he is laughing aloud, really enjoying himself. Yet, in short order, Sol finds himself laughing along with him.

Sol: *(Still laughing.)* You know, sometimes I feel badly for the coyote. Ah, this is just what the doctor ordered. I needed a good laugh.

Iam: Of course. The news is so depressing. You have enough worries now—you need more?

Sol: No, I certainly don't. Oh, my poor wife. Yesterday she woke up with terrible pains in her stomach. I rushed her here, to the emergency room, and they wound up admitting her. I don't know what's going to be. I don't know what to think. *(Beat)* But enough about me. How about you?

Iam: Me?

Sol: Why are you here?

Iam: Oh, I'm just here to help an old friend get through a rough patch.

Sol: That's really nice of you.

Iam: Nah. *(Waves the compliment off in an "Oh, it's nothing really" manner.)*

Sol: No, don't make light of it. People don't always conduct themselves as they ought to. Believe me, I know.

Iam: He may not feel the same way about my visit.

Sol: Nonsense, he's lucky to have you. How about a cup of coffee? I'm buying.

Iam: I prefer tea. Four sugars, please. *(Iam will constantly be drinking tea. After he finishes each cup, he places it at the edge of the table, lined up in a straight row. This odd behavior provokes curious looks from Sol, but he never questions why Iam does this.)*

Sol: Four sugars?

Iam: *(Shrugs)* I have a sweet tooth. *(Sol prepares the tea, pours himself a coffee, serves Iam, and takes a seat beside him on the couch.)* Thank you.

Sol: Oh, by the way, I'm Sol. Sol Green.

Iam: Yes.

Sol: And your name?

Iam: Oh, I've lots of names.

Sol: Is that right?

Iam: Well, I move around, I'm always on the go and a lot of different people call me a lot of different things. But for you, I am Iam.

Sol: Iam? That's an unusual name.

Iam: Yes, it's very unique. It's Hebrew.

Sol: Ah, and of course, my name is Hebrew, too.

Iam: Solomon, like the wise king.

Sol: Yes, but I'm afraid the only thing I have in common with the fabled king is my name.

Iam: You're just being modest. *(He takes a sip of the tea.)* This tea is delicious . . . and I'm finally starting to warm up. *(He shivers.)* It's so cold here.

Sol: Well, it *is* December in New Jersey. I suppose we just have to accept it. What's that old saying? Everyone complains about the weather but no one does anything about it. *(Iam doesn't react to this.)* So, I take it you're not from here.

Iam: Oh, I'm from here, I'm from everywhere. And, at the same time, nowhere. Like I said, I'm always on the move. I just came up from Florida. You know, I think I can finally take this old *shmatah* off. *(He removes his overcoat and drapes it over a chair. Sol is taken aback by Iam's "outfit." Iam is wearing black shoes with white socks that almost meet his plaid Bermuda shorts. He is also sporting an "I Love Florida" tee shirt.)* The weather is beautiful down there this time of year. Not too hot. Not humid. A real pleasure.

Sol: I'm guessing your work keeps you on the go?

Iam: Oy, you've no idea.

Sol: May I ask what line you're in?

Iam: Customer service.

Sol: Oh, boy. I have to say I don't envy you. It must be brutal listening to people's grievances all the time. The customer service department in my company had the highest turnover rate. How long have you been in this field?

Iam: If I told you, you wouldn't believe me.

Sol: Gee, you must have the patience of Job.

Iam: Such a nice fellow.

Sol: Pardon?

Iam: Job. He was "blameless and upright."

Sol: You're well versed in Scripture, I see. I didn't take you for a religious man.

Iam: Does knowing Scripture automatically make one religious?

Sol: No, not necessarily.

Iam: Does my desire to have another tea mean I'm thirsty?

Sol: *(Laughing.)* Not necessarily.

Iam: But I'll have another anyway. This time, *I'm* buying.

Sol: Not for me, thank you. I haven't finished my first. *(Iam shrugs, gets up and prepares his tea as Sol watches. Iam counts out his packs of sugar one by one. The expression on Sol's face suddenly changes from one of amusement to one which suggests a glimmer of recognition. Does he know this peculiar man?)* You know, somehow, you seem oddly familiar.

Iam: Is that so?

Sol: Yes, I feel as if we've met before, but I can't put my finger on when or where.

Iam: Don't think about it and maybe it will come to you.

Sol: Do I seem familiar to you?

Iam: Everyone's familiar to me. *(Takes a big gulp of his tea.)*

Sol: I hope you don't think I'm being rude, that I'm speaking out of turn, but all that sugar—it's very unhealthy.

Iam: For you, maybe.

Sol: For everyone.

Iam: I'm not everyone.

Sol: No, perhaps you aren't. I'm sorry if I offended you.

Iam: Offended? Did you forget what I do? Nah, I'm not so thin-skinned.

Sol: I suppose in today's world none of us could afford to be too sensitive.

Iam: What do you mean?

Sol: Well, take me, for example. I was an orphan, an immigrant who didn't speak a word of English and a lot of people said I didn't have the wherewithal to make it. But by the age of thirty-five, I had built the second largest chain of fine men's clothing stores in the country. I sold my company for more than I ever dreamed possible. Had I listened to the naysayers . . .

Iam: So, you've been successful in business. But success can be measured in other ways.

Sol: That's very profound.

Iam: I have my moments.

Sol: However, the point is, had I been too sensitive—had I listened to those doubters—who knows what would have become of me.

Iam: You wouldn't be married to your wonderful wife? "A wife of noble character—who can find? She is worth more than rubies."

Sol: *(Embarrassed.)* There you go, quoting Scripture again.

Iam: So, sue me.

Sol: Speaking of my wife, I wonder how long this so-called minimally invasive procedure will take. *(Gets up, pokes his head into the hallway looking for someone he can question about his wife.)* These nurses are like cops. You can't find them when you need them. *(Walks over to the beverage bar and pours himself coffee.)* You want another tea?

Iam: I thought you'd never ask. Four sugars, please.

Sol: *(Prepares the drinks, hands Iam his tea, and takes a seat beside him.)* Tell me about your friend.

Iam: Huh?

Sol: The one you're helping through a rough patch.

Iam: Oh, oh, *him*. Well, he's a nice man. He had had a . . . how shall I put it, a difficult childhood. But he managed to build himself a life, a life with a sense of purpose.

Sol: He sounds like a special guy.

Iam: That he is.

Sol: So, what's wrong with him?

Iam: He's about to have a crisis of sorts, a crisis of faith.

Sol: I think that's something most sentient people go though at one time or another. It's not a bad thing. I mean, if, for example, he has questions about the existence of an omnipotent, omniscient entity; why not? It's not at all unusual.

Iam: Don't I know it. But his crisis will be more personal, more of a threat. When a person loses faith in themself, in their own self-worth, they're in danger of losing their essence.

Sol: Again, that's quite profound.

Iam: What could I say? I'm on a roll.

Sol: But wait. How do you know he is *about to* have a crisis and that this crisis *will be* more personal and dangerous?

Iam: I knew you'd pick up on that. Well, right now all I can say is, I just know.

Sol: *(Skeptical.)* Uh, huh. I'm sorry, but if by chance you're right, it sounds to me as if your friend needs a psychiatrist. The psychiatric ward is on the second floor, this is the fifth.

Iam: Some spiritual guidance wouldn't help?

Sol: *(Makes a face of derision.)* Oh, please.

Iam: I see you don't put much stock in the spiritual.

Sol: If that stuff works for you, for your friend, fine. But I—I like to think of myself as a man of reason.

Iam: I see that.

Sol: Before I attended Columbia University for my business degree, I studied philosophy at City College.

Iam: Uh, huh.

Sol: Yes. I learned how to reason and to think logically . . . to have faith in myself. If others want to believe in . . . in their mythologies, well that's their prerogative, but I'm not buying into them. And why should I? If G-d ever existed, he's certainly dead now. He's been dead for a long time.

Iam: Since 1943?

Sol: What? No, no. I'm referring to Nietzsche. Nietzsche died long before. He's the one who originally declared G-d dead.

Iam: Nietzsche, shmeetsy. It was Hegel who first wrote of G-d's death. Friedrich got all the credit.

Sol: *(Taken aback.)* You're full of surprises, aren't you?

Iam: Wait, the best is yet to come.

Sol: Regardless of who said it first, the fact still remains, G-d *is* dead.

Iam: *(Quietly, almost to himself.)* "The reports of my death have been greatly exaggerated."

Sol: What?

Iam: Oh, I was just thinking about something Mark Twain said. Anyway, it was reason that brought you to the conclusion that G-d is dead?

Sol: It was.

Iam: How about Kant?

Sol: What about Kant?

Iam: How about his *Critique of Pure Reason*?

Sol: *(Stammers.)* I, um . . .

Iam: Have you ever heard of Pascal's Wager? He said only an irrational person would choose to live as if G-d did not exist.

Sol: No, but . . .

Iam: Sol, for all your big-shot philosophers with all their fancy-schmancy theories, I could name other big-shot philosophers who also said fancy things. The only problem is they'll contradict each other—they're not compatible. Go ahead, name some philosopher. I don't care what type of philosophy either—metaphysics, epistemology . . .

Sol: *(Getting annoyed.)* What's your point?

Iam: The point is, Sol, with all your faith in reasoning and logic and Nietzsche, you're really no different from your garden-variety theist.

Sol: *(Angry, Iam touched a nerve.)* I most certainly am not. To suggest I could believe in some fairy tale about, about an old man with a long gray beard who looks down on us, who gives a damn about us, who cares if we live or die, if we feel joy or pain is . . . I'd sooner believe in the tooth fairy.

Iam: How about a coffee?

Sol: *(Not hiding his annoyance.)* No, I don't want any coffee.

Iam: *(Gets up and fixes himself another tea. Again, he counts the packs of sugar, one by one. This time, Sol is anything but amused by Iam's behavior. Iam then says the following in a conciliatory manner.)* Look, Sol, all I am saying is the only way you come to believe in *anything* is by the desire, the need, to believe. A belief is a belief. To say one has more merit than another is also based on a belief.

Sol: And that's *your* belief. But I didn't get to where I am by giving credence to fairy tales.

Iam: And where are you, Sol? You're in a hospital in New Jersey along with lots of other people, people from all different backgrounds. If the "fairy tale" beliefs of some help them come to terms with whatever troubles them, while you, with all your reason and logic and your Nietzsche can't, whose beliefs have more value?

Sol: At least I'm not deceiving myself. I'm honest.

Iam: Aren't you? Have you always been honest with yourself, Sol? With others?

Sol: *(After a slight hesitation.)* I have.

Iam: With Ruth?

Sol: *(With this last question, Sol becomes visibly shaken, enraged.)* How do you know my wife's name?

Iam: I know everything about you, Sol.

Sol: Who the hell are you? What do you want with me?

Iam: I must use the washroom. Lots of tea. *(He pats his stomach then exits the waiting room and heads down the corridor toward a bathroom.)*

Sol: *(Sol calls after him.)* Who *are* you? Who the hell *are* you?

Blackout

Scene 2

Sol is pacing in the waiting room and he appears even more upset, more agitated than he did at the beginning of Scene 1. He pounces on Iam when he returns from the bathroom.

Sol: Who are you?

Iam: Whew, I feel better now. But now I'm thirsty. I'm going to have a tea. Would you like a coffee, Sol?

Sol: No, I don't want any damn coffee. What I want is some answers.

Iam: *(Has already started to slowly count his sugars to himself. He lifts a finger and then brings it to his lips, essentially asking Sol to give him a moment of silence until he finishes counting. Sol impatiently obliges. Iam takes a taste of his tea—he's happy with it.)* You were saying, Sol?

Sol: Now, who in G-d's name are you?

Iam: You're invoking the name of a fairy tale character—a *dead* fairytale character—to get answers to your questions, Sol. That doesn't seem very logical. *(Iam stares at Sol, and Sol at him. Iam understands Sol is upset and in no mood to spar with him.)* Sol, I told you. Iam. *(Iam says the following very slowly.)* I am who I am.

Sol: *(Stunned. He looks at Iam incredulously before he breaks out into a roaring, uncontrollable laugh. At long last he says the following, still laughing.)* I can't believe this; you're certifiable. At first I thought you were just a little, a little off, eccentric, especially in that getup. *(Points to Iam's clothing.)* But no, it's off to the second floor for you.

Iam: Sol . . .

Sol: *(Still laughing.)* "I am who I am." Exodus 3:14. Man, this is rich.

Iam: Solomon Green correctly citing Scripture. Your father taught you well. *(With this comment, Sol's laughter comes to an abrupt halt.)*

Sol: What do you know of my father?

Iam: I told you, Sol, I know everything about you.

Sol: Oh, that's right. For a moment I forgot. You're G-d. *(Sol snickers.)*

Iam: Laban Greenberg was born on May 14, 1908, in a small village outside of Gdansk called Jaroslaw. He was a very devout Jew, a rabbi who was admired by all for his quick, encyclopedic mind. Even as a child he outwitted his teachers, asking questions they could not answer. It was said that by age of 12 he could recite the entire Torah by heart. And it was true. Laban walked hunched over. *(Iam demonstrates how.)* Some thought it was because of all the time he spent poring over his books, but he was actually born that way. At age 18—through a matchmaker—he married 16-year-old Leah Weiss. They loved each other very much. Leah ran the family's general store, raised you and your younger sister, Hena . . .

Sol: Okay! Enough! I don't know what you're trying to pull here, mister . . .

Iam: Iam.

Sol: Mister, *("Mister" said slowly, for emphasis.)* but I won't stand for it. Do you really think you could fool me by spouting out a few things about my father? This is the age of the Internet, The Information Age. The only thing I want to know is what you're doing here, what it is you want from me.

Iam: Sol, Sol, think for a minute. As wonderful as your father was, and he *was* quite special, do you really think a poor Jew from a Polish *shtetl* will appear on your fancy-shmancy, super-duper information highway? Do you think it will say how much you despised him? How much you resented him for studying all day while your mother worked? How you blame him for . . .

Sol: *(Shouts.)* Enough!

Iam: Sol, calm down. Maybe you'd like to watch another cartoon. Bugs Bunny is going on now. I love how he outwits that Elmer Fudd guy. He . . .

Sol: Will you *please* leave me alone? I have enough to worry about without your nonsense.

Iam: You're worried about Ruth.

Sol: Of course I'm worried about her—she's my wife.

Iam: You know, she forgave you, Sol.

Sol: Don't you talk about her.

Iam: Oh, it's not to say she doesn't think about Cleveland once in a while, think you might be tempted again. But she does know you love her.

Sol: Nothing happened in Cleveland.

Iam: No, nothing happened. But you were tempted.

Sol: Nothing happened. And I told Ruth everything.

Iam: Well, not exactly everything, Sol. You did, after all, extend your *(Iam makes quotation marks with his fingers)* "business trip" to be with your "lady-friend."

Sol: And nothing happened.

Iam: Yes, Sol, nothing happened. But was it because you had a change of heart or because she never showed?

Sol: *(Sol is shocked Iam knows this. He then continues with an air of resignation—he feels compelled to make his case.)* Ruth and I had been trying to have a baby for years. She miscarried twice in her first term. And then, against medical advice, she . . . she got pregnant again. I was furious. She was risking her life because she was determined to give *me* a child. We had horrible, just horrible, arguments. She said she felt incomplete, something less than a real woman, less than a good wife. I told her she was being silly, that if anything ever happened to her my life wouldn't be worth . . . *(Sol collects himself and then continues.)* Well, to our pleasant surprise her pregnancy was going well. Everything was going fine—until the eighth month. The baby was lost, and the worst part of it was I nearly lost Ruth, too. *(Sol pauses again. He is finding it difficult to continue.)*

Iam: *(Sheepishly)* Maybe a coffee will help.

Sol: *(Looks at him as if to say, "Are you kidding me?")* It took months for Ruth to recuperate physically, but emotionally she was a wreck. She grew distant and angry. I thought . . . I don't know what I thought. The "lady friend" was an independent contractor. We had struck up a friendship. She filled the void at this time, *(he quickly adds)* an *emotional* void—that is, I suppose, even worse than a physical one. I've no real, no acceptable excuse, but I was lost, lonely. You see, I had no one else. I *have* no one else.

Iam: You have me, Sol.

Sol: *(Iam's remark brings a smile to Sol's face.)* Sure, why not? I suppose I do have you. I still think you're about a half bubble off plumb, but you're okay.

Doctor: *(Entering the waiting room.)* Mr. Green, your wife is awake. You can see her for a few minutes, if you wish.

Sol: *(Jumps up.)* Of course. *(He quickly leaves.)*

Iam: *(Calls after Sol.)* Don't worry, Sol, I'll be here when you get back.

Blackout

Scene 3

Iam *is sitting on the waiting room couch drinking a tea and watching Porky Pig sign off with his signature stutter of "That's all folks." Soon after,* **Sol** *enters. Sol looks ashen, forlorn.*

Iam: *(Mimicking Porky Pig.)* That's all folks! *(He laughs, looks at Sol, and asks . . .)* Nu?

Sol: They . . . they found a mass. They took a biopsy and now we have to wait for the results. *(Sits beside Iam.)*

Iam: Yes.

Sol: Ruth's asleep now. But I saw that look in her eyes. It was the same look she gave me when I told her about Cleveland, all those years ago. There's something about that particular look. It's, it's a strange combination of hurt, fear, and . . . I don't know, maybe pity. But strangely, it's not pity for herself—it's . . . for me. Anyway, there's not a damn thing I can do to help—just sit here like a fool and worry.

Iam: I am with you.

Sol: *(Unmoved by Iam's remark, Sol continues.)* You know, in some strange way Cleveland was a godsend. I mean, yes, the whole ordeal was very painful and yet, at the same time, a blessing in disguise. I came dangerously close to losing her, but in the end, when the dust finally settled, we actually grew closer than ever.

Iam: "Godsend?" "Blessing in disguise?" An interesting choice of words.

Sol: *(Warning)* Don't start with me. I'm not in the mood. *(Iam raises his hands, suggesting he will back off. After a beat, Sol says, his voice quaking . . .)* I don't know if I could go on without her. *(After a long pause, Sol continues.)* Like me, you're no spring chicken. I imagine you've suffered losses.

Iam: Of course, Sol. *(Sol looks at Iam inquisitively. He's prodding him to open up, to be more forthcoming. Iam quietly says . . .)* Children, Sol. I've lost children.

Sol: Oh, oh no. I'm *so* sorry. There is no loss more painful than the loss of one's own child.

Iam: No, no there isn't. *(After an uncomfortable silence, Iam turns to Sol and says . . .)* You can use a coffee.

Sol: And you a tea. I'll prepare them.

Iam: Four . . .

Sol: Yes, I remember. Four sugars.

Iam: Of course four sugars. But that's not what I was going to say. Four types of children, Sol. You remember the Passover Seder. It says there are four types of children.

Sol: The wise, the wicked, the simple, and the one who does not know how to ask. What about them?

Iam: There is a another, Sol.

Sol: A fifth? I don't remember a fifth.

Iam: Few ever talk about this child because . . . it's the evil child.

Sol: What's the difference between a wicked and an evil child? They're synonymous.

Iam: The rabbis say a child is wicked who makes the human experience nothing more than an academic exercise by taking himself out of the picture. In this case, it's the Seder and the recounting of a people's redemption.

Sol: I don't think such a child is wicked.

Iam: Of course you don't, Sol. You *are* that child.

Sol: Now, wait a minute now . . .

Iam: Sol, don't tell me that a story that relates acts of divine intervention—miracles—doesn't qualify as . . . how did you put it? Mythology?

Sol: Yes, I suppose I would, but . . .

Iam: Relax, Sol. I know you can be a decent man—your heart is in the right place. I can tell by the way you take care of your children.

Sol: *(Annoyed)* Haven't you been listening to me? I have no children.

Iam: Sure you do, Sol, you have lots of children.

Sol: What are you talking about?

Iam: The Ruth and Solomon Green Foundation. It's mission statement: "Dedicated to the betterment of the lives of people everywhere." Those people, Sol, *they* are your children.

Sol: Having a foundation doesn't make those we try to help *our* children.

Iam: Sure it does, Sol. They don't have to have your DNA

to be yours. Do you know how many people you've helped throughout the years?

Sol: I *am* proud of my charitable work.

Iam: As you should be. And all your . . . *(Looks around, making sure he is not overhead.)* "anonymous" donations.

Sol: Apparently not anonymous enough. How do you know about them? *(Iam gives Sol a look which says, "Really? You want to do this again?")* Oh, right. I forgot with whom I was speaking. *(A beat.)* So, tell me about the fifth child, the evil one.

Iam: Oh, you know enough about evil, Sol; better than most.

Sol: *(Slowly, afraid where this may lead.)* What are you talking about?

Iam: Come now, Sol. You were in Auschwitz for over two years and now you're questioning me about the nature of evil?

Sol: *(Alarmed.)* Stop! Do *not* go there!

Iam: You mean to tell me you forgot about the mounds of naked dead bodies?

Sol: Stop!

Iam: The smell of burnt human flesh?

Sol: Stop!

Iam: The . . .

Sol: Stop! I said stop! I don't need to be reminded of that place. I've spent my life trying to forget it.

Iam: Sol, how could you forget? How could *anyone* who was there forget? Go on, drink your coffee. *(Sol just sits still, staring straight ahead, while Iam greedily devours his tea.)*

Sol: I lost my mother, my kid sister.

Iam: And your father, Sol. Let's not forget your father.

Sol: *(Says the following almost to himself, as if Iam wasn't there.)* To the left. They were sent to the left. My mother and sister were sent to "Bunker One," the gas chamber. They were deemed useless, unable to work in exchange for that inedible garbage they fed us. Of course my father was sent along with them. A weak Jew, hunched over like a question mark. What value did he have to them? What value did he have to anyone? *(A beat)* We could have run. We *should* have run. *(Adds quickly.)* But he was too busy studying to ever live, to take care of his own wife, his own flesh and blood. *He's* the reason they died.

Iam: So, your father was responsible for their death, for his *own* death? Not your neighbor who turned you in? Not the soldiers who packed you into the cattle car? Not the guards who escorted your family to the Zyklon B? Not all the people who turned a blind eye? Oh, I think there's more than enough blame to go around, Sol.

Sol: It was those books, those damn books. We could have run. We had gotten word the Germans were advancing. Maybe, just maybe, if we . . .

Iam: Sol, you've got it wrong. Your father *was* willing to run. It was your *mother* who didn't want to leave—she didn't want to leave the store. Your father was able to continue his studies anywhere. The store—that was a different matter.

Sol: Lies! My father was too busy with his books, too busy praying. The fool. Even after he got off the train and was walking to his death he was still reciting his nonsense.

Iam: It wasn't nonsense, Sol. He said four things that morning. *(Sol looks at Iam inquisitively.)* The first was the *Shema,* the prayer declaring my uniqueness, my oneness. It was greatly appreciated, especially when you consider the circumstances.

Sol: *(Looks at Iam contemptuously.)* I don't have to listen to this crap. *(Sol gets up to leave.)*

Iam: The next was for your mother. *(Sol stops dead in his tracks.)* He recited a Song of Solomon. *(Iam clears his throat and says . . .)*

Song of Solomon, Number Four *(He again clears his throat.)*

Behold, thou art fair, my love; behold thou art fair; thou hast doves' eyes within thy locks: thy hair is a flock of goats that appear from Mount Gilead.

Sol: *(Rolls his eyes.)* Oh, brother.

Iam: Okay, okay, I agree; the thing about the goats doesn't play too well today, but then it continues on to your father's favorite part, the part he would whisper in your mother's ear:

Thou hast ravished my heart, my sister, my spouse; thou hast ravished my heart . . . How much better is thy love than wine . . .

Beautiful, no?

Sol: I don't care what he said, she was too good for him. He didn't deserve her.

Iam: He made her happy, Sol. They understood each other. They loved each other.

Sol: He didn't deserve her!

Iam: Do you deserve Ruth?

Sol: I . . . , that . . . that's different.

Iam: Is it? How so, Sol? *(He waits for an answer, and when none is given, asks . . .)* Coffee?

Sol: *(Shakes his head "no." After a pause, he asks . . .)* What else? What else did he say?

Iam: *(Slowly prepares his tea and answers only after he finishes.)* Sol, your father understood. He *knew* that your mother, sister, and he were not going to, well . . . make it. But he prayed *you* would. He said the three Priestly Blessings for you.

Sol:

May the Lord bless you and guard you,

May the Lord shed light on you and be gracious unto you,

May the Lord give you peace.

Every Friday night, at the beginning of the Sabbath, he would place a hand on my head, his other on Hena's, and bless us. *(A beat)* What's the fourth thing, the fourth thing he said?

Iam: Your father recited Kaddish—the prayer for the

dead—for your sister, for your mother, and then for him-self, because . . . he knew you wouldn't.

Sol: *(Opens his mouth to speak, but nothing comes out.)*

Iam: Even when you were a child he sensed your cyni-cism. When you got older, you made no attempt to hide it. He knew you didn't like him, didn't respect him, *and* that he embarrassed you. Right Sol? You couldn't understand how, why, a hunchback—a physically broken man—could, should receive the respect he was given, let alone your mother's love. He was, how did you put it, Sol, "nothing more than a snake oil salesman whose only stock and trade was lies and superstition."

Sol: *(Defiantly.)* Yes, I said that. And I stand by it. Tell me, what's supposed to happen here? Do you expect me to have a sudden change of heart—an epiphany—and declare my father some kind of saint or something?

Iam: No, Sol. He doesn't need your validation, but it would be nice if you showed him some respect.

Sol: Respect? Respect for going to the gas without a single act of defiance? Every day I watched those trains come. I watched people . . . women and children . . . infants . . . most of them *his* beloved people, get off those trains and quietly, obediently go to their death. You talk about Passover and redemption? You talk about miracles? G-d? Where was G-d then?

Iam: I was there, Sol. And I was there when your father reaffirmed his faith in me. *This* was his act of defiance.

Sol: *(Surprised by Iam's response.)* I'm sorry, I can't do this with you now. I'm just too damn upset to indulge you in your . . . G-d complex or whatever's going on with you.

Iam: 183071

Sol: *(Stunned by Iam's comment. He instinctively grabs his sleeved left arm.)* I . . . how . . . how?

Iam: It's interesting, Sol, don't you think?

Sol: *(Still dazed.)* Huh?

Iam: The mark of mass murderers, of evil, is indelibly emblazoned on your arm, but you found your father so reprehensible you felt compelled to change your name— his name. Greenberg just wouldn't do.

Sol: *(Dismisses Iam's remark, demanding . . .)* How?

Iam: I told you, Sol, I know everything about you. *And,* as I said, I was there.

Sol: *(Excitedly.)* Wait! Wait a minute now. You were there? *You* were *there*? Then where's yours? *(Sol points to Iam's left arm, which bears no tattoo.)*

Iam: I don't have it anymore.

Sol: *(Snidely.)* Oh, I guess it just up and left. The charade is over, my friend. You've been exposed.

Iam: Exposed? No, Sol, revealed. But yes, I am your friend.

Sol: Friend? I have no idea who you are. Would you like some advice as to how to get some friends? Try dressing like a man, not like some crazy kid on spring break.

Iam: Sol, you still haven't learned. You're 69 years old, you've been through a lot, and yet you still have trouble seeing what lies below the surface. Tell me, did the yellow star on your prison uniform define you?

Sol: I didn't exactly choose that for myself.

Iam: No, but you *were* given the ability to decide what type of person you wanted to be. Take your father, Sol. He was born disfigured, but he strove to become the best person he possibly could. He could have easily become a bitter, very disagreeable person, but he chose to be kind and loving instead. It's too bad you couldn't see past his black hat, his black coat, and . . . his deformity. Your mother could, and a man like you—a man of reason—should know better.

Sol: Who are you?

Iam: I told you who I am, Sol. Whether or not you choose to believe me—believe *in* me—is your choice.

Sol: *(Dismissive.)* Yeah, yeah. And *why* are you here?

Iam: I'm here to keep a promise I made.

Sol: What promise?

Iam: Coffee?

Sol: No. What promise?

Iam: *(Has already begun to prepare himself a tea. Once again he is slowly counting his four sugars and Sol knows better than to interrupt him. When he finishes, he takes a big gulp and then says . . .)* I must say, Sol, I am a little disappointed you don't remember me.

Sol: *(Angrily.)* What promise?

Iam: Patience, Sol. I must first visit the washroom. *(Iam leaves. Sol, visibly upset, paces.)*

Blackout

Scene 4

Sol: *(Still pacing, stops, looks up, arms outstretched as if he was petitioning G-d, and asks the following just as Iam returns.)* What did I do to deserve this?

Iam: I'm over here, Sol. *(This comment makes Sol even more upset.)* Now, back to business. You, Sol, are the son of Laban Greenberg, and *his* blessings for *you* have been and will be answered.

Sol: What are you talking about?

Iam: We've been through this, Sol. When your father left the train that morning, he recited the three Priestly Blessings in supplication for you. I promised to fulfill them. The first: "*May the Lord bless you and guard you,*" has already been fulfilled.

Sol: So, *you, you* blessed and guarded me?

Iam: If not me, who then?

Sol: *(Shouting, but Iam remains unfazed by Sol's rant.)* Damn you! Damn you for making me do this you, you crazy bastard! You want to know *who* I have to thank for surviving? Huh? It sure as hell wasn't you. It was a kid, a kid just a few years older than me. Yes, a kid! *He* was the one who changed my work assignment. Instead of working in the crematorium or outside in subzero weather where I wouldn't have lasted a week, *he* got me assigned to the processing center. Oh, don't get me wrong, it was no picnic in there, but compared to what others had to do . . . We, we had to go through, sort the belongings of those poor slobs who every single day came off those trains—like sheep to the slaughter. We collected stacks of eyeglasses, shoes . . . their *hair!* Gold was ripped from their teeth. And you know what their worst loss was? *(He quickly adds.)* And no, it wasn't their lives. No . . . it was their dignity. They were stripped of their dignity. You say I can't see what lies below the surface? I saw people, I saw . . . *(Sol starts to lose it.)* people . . . people robbed of their soul! *That,* that's what this kid saved me from. *(Sol now stares at Iam, in essence challenging him to refute his account.)*

Iam: *(Calmly.)* Now tell the rest of the story, Sol.

Sol: What do you want me to tell you, huh? I survived. I survived until the Russians came and liberated us.

Iam: Tell me, Sol, what became of Eli, the boy who saved you?

Sol: Eli?

Iam: Yes Sol, Eli.

Sol: The kid was a, a scrounger. He had a knack for getting his hands on things we needed to get by. He got us food, clothing, even medicine. *(A beat.)* He was shot dead by one of the guards. He was then cremated.

Iam: And why was he shot and burned, Sol?

Sol: I don't see what this has to do . . .

Iam: *(Firmly.)* Why was he shot and burned, Sol?

Sol: A snitch turned him in, said he was stealing from the guards' quarters. But when they searched him, they found nothing, nothing but four . . .

Iam: Yes, Sol?

Sol: It can't be . . .

Iam: Yes, Sol?

Sol: *(Sol now leans into Iam and examines his face closely.)* It can't possibly be . . .

Iam: What did they find in Eli's pocket, Sol?

Sol: *(Said slowly, eerily calm.)* Four, four cubes of . . . sugar. *(A beat)* But . . . you're dead.

Doctor: *(Enters the waiting room and asks . . .)* Mr. Green, may I have a word with you?

Sol: *(Leaves with the Doctor, but he is staring back over his shoulder at Iam saying . . .)* But you're dead. You're dead.

Blackout

Scene 5

Sol returns from his consultation with the doctor to find Iam on the floor of the waiting room doing a yoga plank. Sol shakes his head in disbelief. Just when he thought things couldn't get any more bizarre . . .

Iam appears to be so engrossed in his exercise that when Sol quietly takes a seat, he believes Iam doesn't know he is there. But when Iam finishes his exercise, he says without looking up at him . . .)

Iam: Hi, Sol. I was just doing a plank I used to do with a Yogi in Tibet. It's good for the core, you know. But never mind that—tell me about Ruth.

Sol: *(Still staring at Iam.)* She was in a lot of pain, even more than before, so the doctor gave her a stronger pain medicine. The pain is caused by a build-up of gas. The gas can't pass because the mass is pressed against the colon. She finally fell asleep, but we still don't have the results of the biopsy. So basically, I don't know much more than I did before.

Iam: *(Without asking, Iam prepares Sol a coffee and places it on the table before him. Sol drinks his coffee as Iam returns to the beverage bar where he, in his typical, ritualistic manner, prepares his tea. Sol's eyes remain fixed on him. Iam then joins Sol on the couch and says . . .)* Try not to worry, Sol.

Sol: Easier said than done.

Iam: Hmm, maybe you'll like this. Marcus Aurelius, the Roman emperor and stoic, said, "Never let the future disturb you. You will meet it, if you have to, with the same weapons of reason which today arm you against the present."

Sol: I don't know. It's proving difficult to be stoic now that reason seems to be failing me.

Iam: How so, Sol? How is reason failing you?

Sol: Well, to begin with, I'm talking to a dead man—a dead man who was cremated, who knows the most intimate details of my life, *and*, get this, claims to be G-d.

Iam: That sounds about right—except the part about me being a man. But let's back up a bit, Sol. If you applied reason to your current state of mind, what conclusions would you reach?

Sol: I'd have to say . . . I must be totally nuts.

Iam: Fair enough. And what else?

Sol: I, I don't know. Being a nut job seems to cover it.

Iam: Sol, think. What's the alternative? If, on one hand, you are, as you say, crazy, then on the other, you are . . .

Sol: . . . sane?

Iam: Correct. And that makes all that's happened between us, all what's happening *now* . . .

Sol: . . . real? I rather doubt that.

Iam: Of course, you do.

Sol: Why shouldn't I? How could I not? How can *anyone* possibly believe this?

Iam: Your father would have. He understood the limitations of reason, Sol. But reason has failed you.

Sol: Oh no, not entirely—because I can prove you're not who you say you are.

Iam: Here we go . . . I was expecting this.

Sol: Do you really want to hear it? Are you up for it?

Iam: Don't beat around the burning bush, Sol. Let me have it.

Sol: *(Sarcastically.)* Cute.

Iam: Ha, you see what I did there? Okay, go on. Give it to me good.

Sol: Well, we don't have to look any further than what we touched on earlier. Evil.

Iam: Okay.

Sol: Now, isn't G-d supposed to be all powerful *and* all good?

Iam: Oh boy. Alright, I'll play along. Yes, Sol, I am both.

Sol: Great. So, how do you explain the existence of evil? Logic dictates everything G-d does *must* be good.

Iam: Theoretically, Sol, you're right. Your argument, your syllogism, is sound.

Sol: I feel a "but" coming on.

Iam: *(Ignores Sol's comment.)* It's basic logic. If both premises are true, the conclusion derived by said premises is inescapable.

Sol: So, because you agree evil does exist, you can't possibly be who you say you are. *And,* get this, *no* entity claiming to be both beneficent and omnipotent could. *(Gloats—he's proud of himself.)* There you are . . . checkmate!

Iam: Very good, Sol. You've done Aristotle and Professor Cimino, your logic teacher, proud. But it is hardly checkmate, it's not even check. But it *is* time for some castling.

Sol: What?

Iam: I'm just extending your chess metaphor, Sol. Castling is when a chess player moves his king and rook . . .

Sol: *(Annoyed.)* I know what castling is.

Iam: Yes. Now do you also know what "good" means?

Sol: *(Insulted by the question.)* You must be kidding.

Iam: Please, Sol, indulge me.

Sol: Okay. It, it means morally right, ah, virtuous, having integrity.

Iam: Nicely done. Now, does everyone have the same morality? Does everyone see virtuosity and integrity the same?

Sol: *(Sees where this is headed.)* I, I suppose not.

Iam: So, you agree the notion of "goodness" is a relative term. It's particular to communities and individuals within a community.

Sol: *(Reluctantly.)* Yes. I get it. I see what you're doing. But I'm sorry, there is no way you can convince me that, that the wanton destruction of life, the cruelty I saw, can be defined as anything other than evil. *(A beat.)* And it never seems to end. How about Darfur, Rwanda, the Khmer Rouge? Shall I go on?

Iam: No, there's no need. There's something else at play though, Sol, something you haven't considered.

Sol: *(Sarcastically.)* This ought to be good.

Iam: It's also something we touched on earlier. Choice. Or as theologians and philosophers like to call it, free will. Tell me, Sol, were you the successful businessman you were because you were fated to be, was it just chance, or did you get where you were through hard work and determination?

Sol: I worked my tail off.

Iam: And that was your choice, Sol. You made choices that helped you to achieve your goal. In philosophical terms, assuming an existential posture, you created yourself. *(A beat.)* Good people do the same. The good I bestowed on man is the good that comes with good choices that free will engenders. Man has the choice—the ability—to *not* exercise the good, but free will is *not* inherently evil.

Sol: Why aren't those who act badly punished?

Iam: Who said they aren't? But having said that, Sol, you need to understand that one's choices, when translated into action—or inaction—invariably impact others. And acts motivated by good intentions won't always result in a beneficent outcome.

Sol: *(After digesting all that Iam has said, he says . . .)* I have another question.

Iam: Only one, Sol?

Sol: The second Priestly Blessing: *May the Lord shed light on you and be gracious unto you.* Well, was my success *really* mine, or was it . . . something else?

Iam: It was me, Sol, at least in the beginning.

Sol: *(Disappointed, he bows his head.)* Oh.

Iam: Yes, I *knew* you and Ruth would hit it off.

Sol: *(Quickly)* But I meant . . .

Iam: . . . I know what you meant, Sol. Yes, your business dealings were your own.

Sol: *(Embarrassed.)* I suppose you think I'm a real jerk thinking about my business, about myself, rather than Ruth.

Iam: Coffee?

Sol: *(Jumps up.)* I'll make them. *(After preparing the drinks, Sol sits down beside Iam and says . . .)* I do have more questions.

Iam: I'm sure you have many more questions you could ask, Sol. And I'm sure they are equally if not more irreverent than the one you posed questioning my benevolence. I only agreed to answer it because of your father, but it *is* rather silly for you to think you could truly understand any *real* explanation I may offer to *any* of your questions. *(A beat.)* Do not presume you are somehow owed *anything*, Sol, and know there is a limit to my patience.

Sol: I'm . . .

Iam: Yes, I'm sorry too, Sol. I'm sorry you experienced what you did, and at such a tender age. I'm sorry you lost your family. And I'm also sorry the third Priestly Blessing has not yet been granted.

Sol: *(Quietly.) May the Lord give you peace.* It's true—I've never felt at peace. With all that I have . . .

Doctor: *(Entering the room.)* Mr. Green, may I speak with you in private, please?

Sol: Whatever you have to say, you can say in front of my friend.

Doctor: Okay. Well, I'm afraid I have some disturbing news. The results of your wife's biopsy came back and I'm afraid the growth is malignant. We are prepping her now for surgery.

Sol: (Sadly.) Oh, may I see her before she goes in?

Doctor: Yes, of course. But please make it quick.

Sol: Okay. *(He quickly leaves.)*

Doctor: *(To Iam.)* Excuse me, you look awfully familiar but I can't place you.

Iam: I get that a lot.

Doctor: Ah. *(The Doctor leaves, but not before he takes a look back at Iam.)*

Blackout

Scene 6

Sol returns to the waiting room but Iam is not there. He appears very worried and quietly, sadly takes a seat. He picks up the remote to the television and increases the volume. The Jetsons *is on. Iam, presumably returning from the washroom, enters. Sol is happy, relieved to see him.*

Iam: There's no doubt about it, Sol, tea *is definitely* a diuretic. Now, tell me about Ruth.

Sol: She's . . . brave. She always has been. *(A beat.)* You know, *she* was the secret of my success. I see that now. *(A brief pause.)* Iam, is it possible . . .

Iam: . . . no, Sol. It's a beautiful gesture, but I'm afraid it doesn't work that way. The third Priestly Blessing, *May the Lord give you peace*, was your father's prayer for you, and for you alone.

Sol *and* Iam *both sit quietly in a comfortable silence. They then start to watch the television, also in silence, until* Sol *says . . .)*

Sol: *The Jetsons.* Who *really* knows what the future has in store for us?

Iam: I do, Sol. Do you see the apparent contradiction between that and free will?

Sol: *(Ignores the question and dreamily says . . .)* In a couple of weeks it will be a brand new year, a brand new millennium—2000. Some say the world will come to an end. And I suppose it will; *for some* anyway. Still, there's a lot I'd like to do. I want to take Ruth on a trip . . . maybe take up painting. You know I *did* paint a little when I was a kid. I wasn't bad either.

Iam: *(Says the following while pointing to the poor, cheap print on the wall.)* I hope you're better than this guy was. *(Both laugh.)*

Sol: *(Still laughing)* Of all the beautiful paintings . . .

Iam: *(Both still laughing.)* His mother thought he was going to be the next Rembrandt, but it does serve a purpose.

Sol: *(Said seriously, but still smiling.)* Yes, I suppose it does. I suppose it does. *(Spots the fish tank.)* Hey, you know we've been so busy gabbing we never noticed the fish tank. The fish are really very beautiful. *(Sol looks closely at the fish, taps on the tank and then says . . .)* We've been here for quite a while and no one has fed them. Do you think it would be alright if I did?

Iam: That would be just fine, Sol.

Sol: *(Takes a pinch of food and sprinkles it on top of the water.)* Look at 'em come. They sure are hungry. Wait, check this one out. I think it's pregnant. *(Sol continues to look at the fish while Iam, sitting calmly, watches on.)* You know, I read somewhere that some fish eat their own offspring. I wonder why.

Iam: An orangutan mother stays in constant physical contact with its baby months after it is born, feeding and caring for it. Talk about different parenting styles. *(Both Sol and Iam laugh.)*

Sol: *(The expression on Sol's face then changes. He asks sadly . . .)* I guess I was a pretty rotten son, wasn't I?

Iam: Why do you suppose that is, Sol?

Sol: I don't know. Maybe it's because my father had so much faith—*too* much faith. He was always so sure things worked out for the best. I couldn't see it. I couldn't understand how he could put so much faith in things that can't be seen, can't be touched.

Iam: Do you believe in love, Sol?

Sol: Yes.

Iam: Even though love can't be seen or touched?

Sol: Yes, but love is different, Iam. Love manifests itself in living, breathing things. I *know* I love Ruth.

Iam: I don't mean to be indelicate here, Sol, but if Ruth should pass away, will your love for her die with her?

Sol: *(Sadly.)* I suppose I would still be in love with the *idea* of her.

Iam: And what's the difference, Sol? *(Iam waits for Sol's response, but when none is given, he continues . . .)* Let me ask you another question: You said your father was always sure things worked out for the best. Did they? Did things work out for your father, Sol?

Sol: Well, like you said, he *was* well respected and he and my mother *did* love each other very much. I guess he was fairly content . . . up until his death, that is.

Iam: Death being an inevitability, a fate *all* people will face.

Sol: Of course. *(A beat.)* What am I to do, Iam? He's gone and I can't tell him . . .

Iam: . . . you're sorry? That you love him?

Sol: *(Sadly.)* Yes.

Iam: The best thing you can do to honor your father now, Sol, is to live, find contentment, find peace. That's all he ever wanted for you.

Sol: *(Starting to break down.)* But why . . .

Iam: Say it, Sol.

Sol: *(Sol can't speak. He shakes his head "no.")*

Iam: *(Slowly and sternly.)* Say it, Sol.

Sol: *(Crying now.)* Why did I survive when, when my father, my mother and sister, and so many others . . . didn't?

Iam: You have so much to be grateful for, Sol.

Sol: I do, but I constantly feel lonely, guilty . . . and so very sad.

Iam: You survived physically, Sol, but your mind and your heart have not healed. I wouldn't attribute your pain to a lack of faith, although faith *would* be helpful. But I will say that none of those around you, Sol, not even Ruth, could possibly fathom, possibly begin to understand all you've experienced. That is why you feel lonely.

Sol: And my guilt?

Iam: Your guilt, Sol, is misdirected. It should not be leveled at your father—and certainly not at yourself. Sol, you are living proof that evil does not prevail.

Sol: Hasn't it?

Iam: No, Sol, it hasn't. You have countered evil with kindness and compassion. You have challenged hatred by embracing life. *(A beat.)* Can I tell you an ancient commentary on the Passover story, Sol?

Sol: *(Half laughing, half sobbing.)* I'd prefer it if you didn't.

Iam: *(Wryly.)* Too bad, I'm going to tell you anyway. *(A beat.)* The Hebrews, in the face of the Pharaoh's decree that all their newborn males be put to death, redoubled their efforts to have children. Now this may seem like irrational, irresponsible behavior, but the ancient Hebrews understood that by *not* having children, they would actually be contributing to their enemy's plan to exterminate them. I'm telling you this, Sol, so you'll understand that sometimes you must look back, see where you've been, so you know where you are headed. Liberation, both personal and in general, is dependent on *never* liberating yourself from your memories, no matter how painful, how difficult that may be.

Sol: *(Wearily.)* I'm tired, Iam. So, very tired . . . Eli.

Iam: I know, Sol. Rest. *(He leads Sol to the couch and helps him sit down.)* Close your eyes, my child. *(Sol closes his eyes and quickly falls asleep. Iam looks at Sol affectionately. Satisfied Sol is now at peace, Iam takes his overcoat and leaves quietly.)*

The house lights momentarily dim, suggesting the passage of time. The Doctor *then enters and finds* Sol *asleep. He gently touches Sol's shoulder, arousing him from his slumber.*

Doctor: Mr. Green, I'm pleased to tell you the surgery went very well. We removed the mass and a part of the affected area and your wife is now cancer-free.

Sol: *(Excitedly.)* Oh, oh! Thank you, doctor . . . I, I don't know what to say—how to thank you.

Doctor: You're quite welcome. Now, I do recommend your wife have some radiation treatments as a precaution, along with regular check-ups. We need to keep an eye on things.

Sol: Yes. Yes, of course. And doctor, the pain? Is my wife out of pain?

Doctor: She is. She is now able to pass gas.

Sol: Iam, did you hear that? Ruth can fart again! *(Sol turns around and realizes Iam isn't there. Sol is unsettled by Iam's absence.)*

Doctor: *(Looks at Sol curiously, then politely says . . .)* Well, I'm very happy for you, Mr. Green. So long, now. *(The two shake hands and the Doctor leaves. Sol then looks around the waiting room in a daze. Sol notices Iam's overcoat is no longer there.)*

Sol: *(To himself, aloud.)* Could it have all been . . . a dream? *(Sol then spots the line of Styrofoam cups on the edge of the table. He smiles to himself. He carefully collects them and places them in the trash. Happy, Sol leaves the waiting room, but not before he says in his best Road Runner voice . . .)* Beep! Beep!

Curtain

CPSIA information can be obtained
at www.ICGtesting.com
Printed in the USA
BVHW01*1156220118
505970BV00005B/13/P

9 780692 048894